TRANS
FUTURES
NOW

TRANS FUTURES NOW

A QUEER GUIDED JOURNAL ON FINDING
YOUR ALLIES, DEMANDING LIBERATION,
AND USING YOUR VOICE

MILO STEWART

mango
PUBLISHING GROUP

CORAL GABLES

Cover Design: Elina Diaz
Layout & Design: Megan Werner

For permission requests, please contact the publisher at:
Mango Publishing Group
2850 S Douglas Road, 4th Floor
Coral Gables, FL 33134 USA
info@mango.bz

For special orders, quantity sales, course adoptions and corporate sales, please email the publisher at sales@mango.bz. For trade and wholesale sales, please contact Ingram Publisher Services at customer.service@ingramcontent.com or +1.800.509.4887.

Trans Futures Now: A Queer Guided Journal on Finding Your Allies, Demanding Liberation, and Using Your Voice

Library of Congress Cataloging-in-Publication number: 2022931239
ISBN: (p) 978-1-64250-846-8 (e) 978-1-64250-847-5
BISAC category code JNF053080, JUVENILE NONFICTION / LGBTQ+

Printed in the United States of America

TABLE OF CONTENTS

HOW TO USE THIS JOURNAL

Hi, I'm Milo. I'm a proud member of the trans community, a vlogger, and your guide for this guide. The goal for this project was to create a resource for people like me and like you to have an outlet. A tool that can help you organize and understand all the emotions and feelings rolling around your mind and body.

So this journal, what is it? It's whatever you need it to be. A friend, a diary, an escape. I hope that the writing prompts, exercises, and resources within the pages help you feel a little more secure. I'll start off by telling you about myself, the history of our community, and the world we're aiming to shape. And hopefully by the end of the journal, you'll have told me all about yourself too.

Our history has been censored in the past. Be it by religion or politics or just hatred, the truth is that trans truths have never been fully told. For every step we take forward, someone is always there to say it didn't happen. So I hope these next few sections help change that. I wanted to include my story and tipping points as a way to say that all our journeys matter. And that our struggles should be documented, even if just in a journal for now.

RESOURCES

Before you start using this journal, I think it will be helpful to have
a few resources at your disposal. If not for you, for someone who
you care about.

Transgender people in crisis should contact the following resources:

1. The Trevor Project's 24/7/365 Lifeline at 866-4-U-TREVOR
    (866-488-7386) or TrevorChat, their online instant messaging
    option, or TrevorText, a text-based support option.

2. If you are looking for peer support, you can visit TrevorSpace
    from anywhere in the world.

3. The National Suicide Prevention Lifeline at 800-273-TALK
    (8255) Trans Lifeline at 877-565-8860.

4. Do you live outside the United States? If so, check out The
    Trevor Project's list of international resources here:

    -   Transgender Organizations National Center for
        Transgender Equality (NCTE) (advocacy)

    -   Transgender Legal Defense and Education Fund (TLDEF)
        (legal services)

    -   Transgender Law Center (TLC) (legal services
        and advocacy)

    -   Sylvia Rivera Law Project (SRLP) (legal services)

    -   Trans People of Color Coalition (TPOCC) (advocacy)

    -   Trans Women of Color Collective (TWOCC) (advocacy)

    -   Black Trans Advocacy (advocacy)

- Trans Latina Coalition (advocacy)

- Gender Spectrum (support for families, trans youth, and educators)

- Gender Diversity and TransFamilies (support for families, trans youth, and educators)

- Trans Youth Equality Federation (support for families and trans youth)

- TransTech Social Enterprises (economic empowerment)

- SPART*A (advocacy for trans military service members)

- Transgender American Veterans Association (advocacy for trans veterans)

- TransAthlete.com (info about trans athletes)

- Massachusetts Transgender Political Coalition (MTPC) (advocacy)

- TransLife Center at Chicago House (support services)

- Trans Doe Task Force (legal services)

These are just some of the incredible outlets that GLAAD has outlined on their website. You can learn more and find an even bigger part of our community here: www.glaad.org/transgender/resources.

INTRODUCTION

I will never forget the feeling of meeting a trans person in real life
for the first time. I was in 8th grade, identifying as pansexual at the
time, and hadn't started to question my gender. Some unconscious
curiosity I hadn't identified within me was piqued by a conversation
I overheard in the halls of my 8th and 9th grade middle school in
Ankeny Iowa.

I later learned the student walking in front of me identified as
a trans man and was taking testosterone as a 9th grader. I was
drawn into his conversation by some word—Was it "gender"? Or
"transgender"?—so deeply that I walked past my next class by
mistake. That interaction (or lack thereof) stuck in my mind for
days and prompted later Google searches that led me to finding the
YouTube channels of trans men making videos to document their
lives and transition—creators like Alex Bertie, Ryan Cassata, and
Chase Ross. It was a few months after finding and binge-watching
Alex Bertie's videos that I first called myself "genderqueer," then
switching to "transgender," before adding on "nonbinary."

The meaning this story holds for me demonstrates the power in being
able to look up to another trans person. I was vaguely aware of trans
people's existence before this interaction, but meeting a trans guy at
my school opened a new world for me as I learned that trans people
exist in the mundane of every day, living lives that aren't exclusively
full of suffering as they appeared to in TV and movies I had seen. In
this way, every trans person owes their ability to claim an identity to
the wider community. We breathe each other into existence by way
of showing how to externalize the feelings that we only felt internally
before learning from example. We don't do this in the way that trans-

exclusionary radical feminists (TERFs) would like people to believe, that trans adults prey on the insecurities of young children to make them change sexes (I hyperbolize, but that isn't far from how TERFs see trans people). Learning that being trans is possible and joyful didn't suddenly make me choose to be a different gender than the sex I was assigned at birth; finding the community around the term "trans" put into the world all of the feelings that were already inside of me. We show each other (as well as cisgender, or non-transgender, people) that there is another way of existing. We can choose to transition and label our genders for ourselves, and, beyond that, the way that we understand gender can change the ways we relate to every person we interact with every day.

In this way, claiming a trans identity puts you in conversation with all other trans people. The terms that we use to describe ourselves change constantly as a result of being forced to forge our identities out of a binary, biological script handed down to us by doctors and relatives who are unaware of the violence these systems create. I'm regularly learning new ideas that challenge my understanding of gender identity when talking to friends and reading academic journals. I imagine that most trans people are doing the same. In the US, there are an estimated 1.4 million trans adults[1] (but like...we know that this number is higher because of the many reasons trans people may not want to or be able to self-identify). We are always updating the meanings of terms as we learn more and coining words that fit us better than the options presented to us. We're not always in consensus about how to talk about our shared experiences, let alone who actually "counts" as trans (spoiler: you "count" if you feel trans). The trans community and, in fact, all understandings of gender, are full of contradictions. That is not something that can or should be avoided. There is immense value in becoming comfortable with

1   williamsinstitute.law.ucla.edu/publications/trans-adults-united-states.

what is undetermined. While we may be able to create more unity by parsing out a guided understanding of what forms our community, answering that question will only create more contradictions.

We must accept this fact as a community and, additionally, look toward what can move the liberation of our community forward beyond advancements in language and the visibility of our community. To do so, we must understand the importance of being a part of a shared struggle to begin with. Some consensus, although flexible, is necessary to articulate our needs and build bonds with one another that are vital to healing and making rough political struggles sustainable until the end. Beyond this point, there is an even greater challenge to agree upon what is needed to free us and how we achieve those goals. Both issues, defining ourselves and our political goals, fundamentally deal with the question of "what does trans existence look like—not just existing to fit in and be tolerated, but existing by thriving, by navigating gender (or one's lack of gender) without limits?" The struggle for trans rights exists at both very microscopic and very macro levels. The ability for a nonbinary trans person to seek out top surgery where one chooses to have a flat chest and no nipples (to be tattooed on later in the shape of hearts) tells us about trans freedom, as does a trans person's right to not be fired for being trans. Or, heck, the right of trans people to be able to live and be housed without needing an income (yep, it's about to be that kind of journal...the author voted for Bernie Sanders).

The following pages are an attempt at countering several micro and macro problems facing the trans community The path forward is paved by many proposals like this. I am not the first and should not be the last to imagine what it takes to move forward. Our works build upon and critique each other, so I offer the contributions I have gathered from my life experiences to be critiqued and made into something better.

And, I hope, I also offer levity to oftentimes heavy subjects. Even though cis comedy writers struggle to find them, there are surprisingly many funny aspects to being trans. Few cis people have ever been able to say, "I accidentally left my dick at my parents' house," as I did once when my packer failed to make its way back into my suitcase after a trip home.[2]

My understanding of gender perhaps is most readily judged through the ways that I describe my own gender. To most people, I am both nonbinary and transgender. I use nonbinary to mean that I am neither entirely male nor entirely female—although I don't think my experiences include any "maleness" or "femaleness." And transgender, because the doctor who delivered me didn't put "nonbinary" on my birth certificate. A trans person is anyone whose gender identity doesn't align with the sex they were assigned at birth. That's the easiest way to explain my identity, but that still has its faults. What exactly does it mean for a gender identity and a sex to align? Does the entire community need to be defined in relation to the sexes we were assigned at birth? What is sex, and what does it actually tell us about a person? Oof! We're looking at a lot of issues!

I think of myself in terms that describe me better than "trans" and "nonbinary," but I don't often use these to introduce myself. I do ask that other people refer to me using they/them pronouns or alternate between binary pronouns when speaking in a language without a singular gender-neutral pronoun. I also love "genderfucked," "gender creative," "gender expansive," and any way of labeling the fact that I feel *a lot* of gender and enjoy experiencing it. Does it make sense to describe a gender identity in terms of quantities? The only similar term might be "agender," describing someone who doesn't have a gender, which is on another side of the gender spectrum, if gender were described by quantity. I have all of the gender, and, simultaneously, all of the distinct

2   A packer is a prosthetic penis worn to give the look and feel of having a bulge.

TRANS FUTURES NOW

genders within me lose their meaning by virtue of existing within me at once. If I am to give a more tangible description of this experience, I'd say that no labels for gender make complete sense with my experiences, but I enjoy replicating selective, performative elements of both binary genders in addition to nonbinary subcultures. It's ok if this doesn't make sense to you! The specificity of how every individual feels in their gender matters more for the micro level of personal freedoms than it does for the macro level of how systems need to be destroyed and rebuilt to accommodate diverse experiences with gender.

Beyond gender, I also identify as a grey-asexual, bisexual, leftist, able-bodied, middle class, not formerly incarcerated, white person living in Chicago with US citizenship. My privileges point out how my experiences as a trans person are different from (read: easier) those of poor trans people, trans women, trans people of color, and folks at the intersection of more than two identities. They also explain why my voice is listened to more than others, giving me the opportunity to be published.

Among other experiences that have given me the chance to understand the true, dehumanizing nature of transphobia, I struggled for years for acceptance of my trans identity from friends and family. I came out publicly while I was attending high school in a largely upper-middle-class suburb of Houston (yes, my parents really moved our family including my trans self to Texas after my freshman year). In school, I dealt with horrible transphobia expressed behind my back and to my face, and I was humiliated by institutional transphobia, such as when I was forced to sit in a meeting with my school's principal to argue for my right to use the bathroom of my choice. I'm sorry, but I was too far into the whole "transition to get the gross parts of puberty" track (yay, butt hair!) for a little pee on the toilet seat to convince me that I wanted to waive my human rights. My principal did in fact try to tell me that I wouldn't want to use the men's bathroom because of toilet seat pee. How infantilizing! Trust me, I know men can be gross!

As a senior in high school, my YouTube channel, where I talk about my identity, started being shared among alt-right forums and YouTube channels upset by my politics and loud declaration of my nonbinary identity. A clip from a video where I explained that there are potentially as many genders as people alive—since we all relate to labels differently—was taken out of context and turned into a meme to make transphobic jokes. The notoriously "evil" site Kiwi Farms discusses everything I post on social media five years after I first went viral, referring to me by my deadname and misgendering me as "she" or "it."

Every trans person has their horror stories. Trans bodies still spark too much curiosity, shock, and "moral panic" within many cisgender people that only immense wealth can protect trans people from all situations where others' perceptions of our bodies and expressions put us in danger. The resources that I found when I was first coming out around 2012–2013 were filled with warnings that made it impossible to forget that fact.

I believe there's a wonderful transition (not of the gender variety) happening around how trans communities envision safety and comfort. While the first videos about transition (the gender kind) that I watched on YouTube emphasized the importance of "passing," or being read as the correct gender, and being stealth, or cis-assumed, myself and other nonbinary people presenting their experiences online demonstrate ways to find joy in being visibly trans. Not all trans people will find this comfortable, but for those for whom passing is as constricting as presenting as their birth-assigned sex, trans futures require us to drop all restraints binding us to the script of cisgender experiences.[3] Doing so will liberate trans people to the pleasure of doing gender without fear.

---

3   By the "cisgender script" I'm referring to elements of cisnormativity that trans gender people are expected to play into when we come out, such as making sure our identities, pronouns, expressions, and bodies align within the expectations of one binary gender.

DESCRIBE THE FIRST TIME YOU MET OR FIRST SAW ANOTHER TRANS PERSON. WAS THE MOMENT AS IMPACTFUL FOR YOU AS IT WAS FOR ME? WHY OR WHY NOT?

WHAT ARE SOME WORDS YOU USE TO DESCRIBE YOUR
GENDER (OR YOURSELF) NOW? WHAT ARE SOME WORDS
YOU'RE INTRIGUED BY?

_____

_____

_____

_____

_____

_____

_____

_____

_____

_____

_____

_____

_____

_____

_____

_____

_____

_____

_____

_____

_____

PERSONAL TRANS TIPPING POINTS

Moving from viewing trans existence as membership within a community to a political movement is a contentious goal and one with many challenges. Yet, bringing together people of trans experience in this way is necessary to better the lives of all trans people and achieve the undefined "liberation" that the more politically engaged portions of the community demand over other goals, such as acceptance or tolerance. I don't want to just be *tolerated*, as if the best I could ask is for the people in my life to endure being around a trans person. Being tolerated feels like when I've been told by someone in a position of authority over me, "Sorry, I'm working on calling you they, it's just hard to not think of you as a girl!" Yes, that has happened regularly since I started going by pronouns other than she/her, and my physical transition hasn't made it happen any less. By reading the subtext of that interaction, I felt like she was telling me "I don't really want to call you by your pronouns, so I'm going to pretend I'm trying so I don't have to directly tell you that." Ouch! What a way to communicate that I'm burdening you and you're feigning politeness only as much as you need to just *put up* with me. And I can't forget about the teacher in high school who pulled me aside on the first day of class to ask me about what surgeries I'm getting and then proceeded to misgender me the rest of the school year! It's not fun answering invasive questions just to feel like I made no progress, because exposing my personal experiences didn't translate into any better understanding.

"Acceptance" doesn't even encapsulate the celebration of trans experiences needed to see that trans lives are valuable, and thus, we should not only remove all restrictive barriers preventing trans people from accessing healthy, financially stable supportive communities, safe from violence and incarceration, but also rework institutions and societal norms that treat cisgender and gender-conforming people as the default. I don't *just* want to be called by the correct pronouns and then say "That's it! I no longer need to fight for my rights!" Being accepted as the gender I am by the people in my life doesn't necessarily translate into systemic equality. Even with a caring, trans-affirming support network, a trans person could still run into barriers trying to medically transition and update their legal name and gender marker changes, for instance. Even once I moved to Chicago for college and found an undergraduate program where my professors and classmates almost universally used my correct pronouns and celebrated the fact that I applied class discussions to trans-specific experiences (my major was Peace, Justice and Conflict studies, so social movements and systemic violence were always relevant), I would often be late returning to class after our fifteen minute break, because I had to walk across the street and go into a different building to find the nearest gender-neutral bathroom. While I was lucky to have access to a gender-neutral bathroom at all, it felt degrading to not have the same access to basic infrastructure as students who easily fit into a cisnormative binary gender category, making me lose out on part of the lecture that I was going thousands of dollars into debt to attend.

While it's easy to say what conditions don't allow trans people to live up to their fullest potential, it's harder to say what would make trans people completely free. It will come to the surprise of no one who has met more than a handful of trans people in their lives to hear that trans people don't view safety for themselves in the exact same way as every other member of the community. For many trans people, the best way they can seek safety is by making their transness invisible—changing their appearance to fit into cisgender expectations of gender through passing[4] and staying stealth[5] in all public aspects of life. Although some trans people feel most affirmed in their identities when they can fully fit into the gender performance that is most affirming to them, this choice is often made for one's comfort and as a precaution against potential discrimination or violence, when one might otherwise enjoy being openly trans if it was safer to do so. It is a survival strategy that many trans people cannot escape; being unable to vocalize one's identity and needs comes at the expense of being able to make meaningful changes that could reduce trans peoples' need to rely on survival strategies, leaving many trans people in limbo and on the never-ending verge of losing one's community, income, and housing. When it's safest to hide, communities learn to live with dehumanizing bureaucratic processes because outing oneself to call attention to injustice comes at too high of a risk. Moreover, a trans person who is able to be stealth twenty-four seven and has finished all legal, social, and medical transition that they desire has already passed through many hoops to get to where they are and are less likely to run into the same types of transphobia as someone who can't apply for a lease without being outed as trans because their name and gender marker don't match their presentation. Given these conditions, it's unsurprising that trans people disagree on the way forward for trans futures. Not to mention, the transphobia a person faces varies greatly based on their race, geographic location, experience of (or exemption from) transmisogyny,[6] and ability/disability, so finding a

---

4   "Passing" refers to the experience of a transgender person, usually of a binary gender identity, being read as the gender that they are. For example, a trans man is passing when the cashier at the grocery store calls him "sir."

5   By being "stealth" a trans person outwardly presents as their gender without publicly identifying as trans.

6   "Transmisogyny" refers to the intersection of misogyny and transphobia faced by trans women and transfeminine people. It does not apply to every individual who may experience misogyny and transphobia.

path forward requires a collaborative approach with voices from all of these intersections.

A look at the history of trans existence and activism gives an insightful window into what trans people are up against today and what organizing strategies are effective. In 1987, over a decade before I was born, Sandy Stone published the essay "The Empire Strikes Back: A Posttranssexual Manifesto," which was a response to a violently transphobic book published by Janice Raymond (or that's how I would classify it—I would encourage you to check it out from a library if you want to see for yourself). In her essay, Stone details how trans people have not been able to define our own identities because trans people have been forced to fit into hilariously inaccurate criteria determining who gets to transition and how, which was originally (and largely is still in the present day) prescribed by cisgender male psychologists and surgeons. To break away from this repetitive history, Stone proposes "constituting transsexuals not as a class or problematic 'third gender,' but rather as a *genre*—a set of embodied texts whose potential for productive disruption of structured sexualities and spectra of desire has yet to be explored. In order to effect this, the genre of visible transsexuals must grow by recruiting members from the class of invisible ones."[7] As a way to combat rhetoric about trans women invading women's spaces, an argument that gatekeeps trans women not only from accessing public spaces but also the linguistic and social category of "women," Stone argues that rather than constituting a separate, pathologized, and therefore falsified experience of womanhood, trans women are women who experience gender through transness as opposed to a cisgender experience, and this reframing would allow trans people the freedom to define ourselves for ourselves. To do so, trans people would have to forgo the safety of being stealth in favor of loudly

---

7   sandystone.com/empire-strikes-back.pdf.

proclaiming their self-determined experiences. Essentially, visibility is Stone's solution as the false narratives that have been constructed have been a result of trans people's relative invisibility. (I say relative because trans people came into the public eye only enough to medically transition and live as their correct gender, but not enough to challenge false ideas about trans experiences in the mainstream.)

Stone's article has been critical to my political growth as an organizer, because it provides a window into the ways that the status of trans rights has both changed and stayed the same. As for our successes, trans people have gained an incredible amount of visibility both in the media and in our personal lives, as the increased awareness for trans identities has translated into a greater ability for trans people to "live as" their genders without necessarily having to be stealth, albeit still at great personal risk in many cases. This is truly a step forward, although I can't help but feel as if it's too little change being made at too slow of a pace. To say that is not to discredit the work of the organizers and martyrs who got us as far as we are but to take our wins and energetically call for leaders to expand our goals. It's time to reinvigorate concern for the issues Stone puts forth, particularly how the trans community's lack of collective self-determination has translated into the creation of a category that names the "correct" way to be trans, which designates which trans people are permitted access to medical transition that can allow us to "pass" and thus have an easier time securing housing and employment. With greater self-determination, it could even become more feasible to live as a trans or nonbinary person without trying to pass, to wish to be seen as one's correct gender without necessarily having to be seen as cis. Could it be possible for a trans man to live his life effortlessly as a man without being assumed to be cis? What would it mean for societal understandings of gender if the words "man" and "woman" didn't come with the default assumptions of being cisgender?

Living through a new boom of trans representation on screen and in the media is truly a privilege that I can't ignore, despite the fact that media depictions paint a different picture than what most trans people live through every day. When I first learned what it meant to be transgender (and immediately felt an unexplainable curiosity about transness even though I was probably in elementary school), it was through watching a story about Chaz Bono on *Entertainment Tonight*, which was my small window into celebrity culture without having cable or a computer in my home. If my family was aware of trans people's existence at the time, it was never a conversation topic. Transness was the unspoken possibility of my future, and, because it was unspoken, I felt embarrassed and kept my questioning private when I started watching trans YouTubers, thinking "maybe this could be me."

I got lucky, though, that by the time I was starting to come out, I had shows like *Orange Is the New Black* and *Sense8* to watch where trans actors played trans characters. I know that without this slightly improving visibility of trans people on screen, it would have been harder to brave coming out at my Texas high school. Even though I know there's some inherent risk any time I come out in a conversation, I can at least use the shorthand "trans" instead of "transgender" and be understood, because most people around me have at least a basic understanding of what it means to be trans, leaving less of the educating for me to do.

However, the growth of trans representation on screen hasn't universally shown improvements in trans rights and freedom even just within the US. Greater visibility in this respect has become a double-edged sword; with improvements in education and greater awareness of trans people comes more accessibility of targets to their transphobic harassers. As trans people have become more visible, so have people with deeply ingrained transphobia. In 2014, *Time* magazine published an article called "The Transgender Tipping Point" with Laverne Cox on the cover of the issue.[8] The article emphasized the radical increase of trans representation while also noting the violence and discrimination that trans people are subject to.

This article was widely celebrated by trans people and allies. I even cited it when I competed at national-level high school speech and debate tournaments in 2015—2016, where I competed with a ten-minute original oratory about gender roles and trans liberation supported by my own experiences as a trans person. Seeing trans people in the media gave me hope. In retrospect, I can see how the tipping point the article points to, where transgender identities suddenly became a global issue, ironically marked the start of my most public experiences with transphobia and harassment. At the same time, for the cis people around me, the trans media boom was a chance for greater awareness but also inspired complacency: they didn't necessarily grasp the need for change beyond education. Because my parents happen to be the cisgender people whom I've spent the most time with and have known before the trans media boom, I have seen this contrast most in my relationship with them. While my parents were learning how to love and support a trans child (and making a ton of progress quickly!), I was walking through a daily hell of transphobia.

8   time.com/135480/transgender-tipping-point.

WHAT ARE SOME OF YOUR FAVORITE PIECES OF MEDIA
(YOUTUBE VIDEOS, SHOWS, MOVIES, BOOKS, ETC.) WITH
TRANS REPRESENTATION? IS THERE ANYONE YOU WANT
TO WATCH THEM WITH? IS THERE ANYONE YOU MIGHT
SUGGEST SHOULD WATCH THEM ON THEIR OWN?

AN EXERCISE IN COMING OUT WHEN YOU'RE READY

My parents didn't get a ton of warning that they would have a trans kid. Although I came into a trans identity at twelve, I hadn't presented any super obvious signs to my parents, like resisting wearing dresses or the color pink. In fact, I chose to paint my childhood bedroom the same shade of pink as my solid corduroy duvet cover. So when I started testing the water by bringing up trans identities to them, I got the brunt of the transphobia that had been ingrained in them over fifty years of consuming transphobic media and living in a cisnormative society. I say all this because, while I had a lot of hard, painful conversations with my parents before and soon after coming out, my parents are human. I don't blame them for the ways that they were unprepared to love their child for being trans. I was just lucky that I came into my identity before I had to confront transphobia.

When I was in eighth grade (so we're talking 2012–2013), my mom found out by accident that I was dating a transgender boy. I should say that this was just before I came out to her as genderqueer (the first of many labels I tried on). Even though I had been forbidden from dating until after I graduated high school (sorry mom, that was never going to work), she patiently asked me about how we'd met and what he was like. I remember her saying "I don't understand why you would want to date a transgender person."

She had no way of knowing that I was beginning to question my own gender. I know that the punchline of every joke about trans people before 2010 was about our supposed undesirability, so I don't think she was alone in her worry about me having this type of queer relationship. I have heard from some trans friends that some parents' first worries are how transitioning will affect their child's ability to find a significant other. Still, hearing this assumption about trans people being undesirable vocalized confirmed my internal anxiety that the surgeries I was secretly wishing for would make my body freaky and ruin my chances of being happy.

I'm hesitant to share this story because I don't believe it reflects my mom's opinions, and I prefer to focus on trans joy rather than transphobia and suffering. I love my mom, and any awkwardness that took place when I was coming out to her is all water under the bridge. I recall a conversation about my bisexuality in which she said the label seemed to fit how accepting I am, especially of trans people. She has been a major figure in helping me transition. Our relationship is a testament to how relationships can grow stronger through hard conversations. We had uncomfortable moments because I was able to be open with my mom, and her honesty about her hesitancies with my transness allowed me to help her learn. At the same time, I think parents reading this should hear that you can accidently hurt your trans child. To avoid this as much as possible, educate yourself and work on your relationship with your child like my mom did.

I've always been able to talk fairly openly with my mom. She supported me through some of the most intimate parts of my early transition. In high school, she took me to a store in Houston owned by a queer couple that provided makeovers and gender gear to trans people, where she bought me several binders[9] and smiled awkwardly while the store owner demonstrated how to sew a pouch into a pair of boxer briefs for a packer. She saw how I reacted to these affirming experiences and how necessary they were; she could see that being

9   A binder is an undergarment worn to compress one's chest for a flatter look.

trans isn't something that I can change, and I am happier when I'm able to perform gender the way I want to, physically and socially.

Two years ago, I worked myself up to make a phone call that I'd been putting off. I called my mom from a coffee shop to tell her that I was seeking a consultation for top surgery, and I wanted to ask if I could cover it with her insurance/HSA and if she would stay at my apartment to help me recover. She had said yes to both, despite her deep-rooted aversion to medical intervention that isn't 100 percent medically necessary, which had been her primary reservation since I came out to her as trans. Seriously, I didn't even learn how to swallow pills until I was twenty-two because taking medicine in my family was reserved for fever reducers and the liquid painkillers I had after my wisdom teeth were pulled. My mom wasn't able to help me recover from top surgery because my surgery was in July of 2020, and my mom would have had to fly and risk COVID-19 to help. Still, I wouldn't have been able to get top surgery without her help navigating billing.

My coming out experience with my dad, on the other hand, went very differently. My dad has been the parent I go to when I want to do fun things that my mom would say "no" to, but he hasn't been the first person who I go to for emotional support. So, I literally came out to him by texting him "I'm trans" with no other explanation. He was in the house with me at the time, so he came into my room to give me a hug without talking about my coming out at all. I didn't feel able to tell him more about my identity or dysphoria, and it seemed to me like he didn't know what questions to ask or how to ask them. When I talked to my dad in preparation for writing this chapter, he told me that he felt like he was educated on transness before the media boom, in particular from watching tennis player Renée Richards come out in the '70s, but he was again drawn into the trans media buzz when Caitlyn Jenner came out. In many ways, I feel as though the media representation in 2014—2015 facilitated my dad's understanding of my transness. Even though he'd been exposed to trans media before, the media he was exposed to more recently updated (if not expanded) his understanding, and it spared me from having a lot of conversations with my dad about things that I was not ready to tell him.

He went from heavily resisting using my new pronouns to finding meaningful ways to signal that he supported me over a few years. I first remember feeling like my dad accepted me as not a girl (I was identifying publicly as a trans guy, so not nonbinary yet) when he gave me a greeting card that had "to a cool dude" printed on the inside. Later on, I got a sense of just how strongly media representation of trans people had affected him. I was at my parents' house over winter break of my freshman year of college when my dad told my mom he had something exciting to share at dinner that he hyped up all day. He pulled out a copy of the *National Geographic* "Gender Revolution" issue, with a nine-year-old trans girl on the cover. He began crying while he held it up, and we hugged in a rare emotional moment.

I hope that these stories show how positive trans visibility can be. People can tend toward bigotry due to their distance from the people affected by their assumptions and stereotyping. Trans people on TV bring a new community into the living rooms of average people. This kind of exposure can make dinner table conversations more thoughtful, because those around the table can see the impact of their words on real people.

But with visibility often comes vulnerability. I found that to be true in 2016 when I realized that the word "trans" would also drive clicks from transphobic audiences. Although I'd been making videos about being trans ever since I came out, it wasn't until 2016 that my videos began getting exposed to far-right audiences, drawing a hate viewership to my channel that brought in at least 30,000 views to all my videos, with ratings around 90 percent dislikes. My comments were flooded with trolls typing in all caps:

THERE'S ONLY TWO GENDERS

These were alongside others spamming "Trump 2016." Greater trans visibility had suddenly translated into Trump supporters opposing my gender identity as part of their political platform.

While others around me were sensing a growing trans acceptance, I felt the most targeted I had ever been since coming into my trans identity. I was hit with emotional whiplash: Simultaneously I was receiving congratulations by cis adults for having broken barriers by coming out at my high school and on the national speech and debate circuit while I was being targeted by an angry online hate mob that translated into real life paranoia, hypervigilance, and fear for my safety. Those without firsthand experience of violent transphobia might expect that fully welcoming trans people into their communities would remove all, or at least significant, barriers to trans people. For me, the growing trans visibility felt like a massive crescendo, clashing with the vulnerability of suddenly hearing *everyone's* opinions on my existence, most with the background of only having thought critically (and abstractly) about the existence of trans people for a few months.

WHEN AND HOW DID YOU BEGIN QUESTIONING YOUR "ASSIGNED" GENDER? WHAT DID THAT FEEL LIKE? IF YOU HAVEN'T EVER QUESTIONED YOUR "ASSIGNED" GENDER, HOW DO YOU KNOW THAT YOU ARE YOUR GENDER?

_____

_____

_____

_____

_____

_____

_____

_____

_____

_____

_____

_____

_____

_____

_____

_____

_____

_____

_____

_____

_____

HOW HAVE YOUR FAMILY AND FRIENDS GROWN IN THEIR
UNDERSTANDING OF TRANS IDENTITIES AND THE ISSUES
THAT TRANS PEOPLE FACE? WHAT GROWING DO THEY STILL
HAVE TO DO?

_____

_____

_____

_____

_____

_____

_____

_____

_____

_____

_____

_____

_____

_____

_____

_____

_____

_____

WRITING PROMPTS

That's me. That's my story. Like everyone's in our community, it's unique and scary and exciting and filled with uncertainty. But, at the end of the day, it's one that is representative, in some way, of all of us. We need to find our voices to not just express the general struggles, bodily changes, and awkwardness, but also the very real fear of being shunned, exiled, or worse. But that's why having this community is so important. Knowing that we're not alone is such a resource that we cannot take for granted. It is something I wish my younger self would have really understood. With that in mind, for the remainder of this journal, I hope to guide you as you explore everything that you feel and connect you to the trans community. Really use these writing prompts, not as school assignments for a grade, but as a form of art. A way to express yourself.

WRITE A LETTER TO YOUR PAST SELF. A LETTER TO FIVE-
YEAR-OLD YOU. A LETTER THAT LETS THEM KNOW THE
JOURNEY YOU'VE BEEN ON. THE DIFFICULT PARTS, THE PARTS
THAT SEEMED LIKE THEY WOULD NEVER GET BETTER, AND
THEN MOMENTS THAT HAVE BEEN WORTH CELEBRATING.

WRITE ABOUT YOUR SUPERPOWER. WE ALL HAVE ONE. FOR THE TRANS COMMUNITY, ONE SUPERPOWER WE NEED TO HONE IS OUR ABILITY TO COPE WITH THE CHALLENGES OF BEING VISIBLE OR FIGHTING OUR INVISIBILITY. EXAMINE HOW YOU WORK TO MAKE YOURSELF VISIBLE (IF YOU'RE READY FOR THIS) AND THE HURDLES THAT COME WITH FLEXING THIS MUSCLE.

CREATIVITY IS A WONDERFUL TOOL TO USE WHEN YOU NEED TO CLEAR YOUR MIND. FOR THIS EXERCISE, TRY TELLING YOUR FAVORITE STORY RELATED TO THE TRANS COMMUNITY WITH DIFFERENT WORDS. IT COULD BE YOUR STORY OF COMING OUT OR BEING THE SHOULDER A FRIEND LEANED ON WHEN THEY WERE STRUGGLING WITH THEIR JOURNEY. INSTEAD OF USING REGULAR WORDS, TRY REPLACING ALL THE EMOTIONS IN THE STORY WITH COLORS OR SOUNDS.

EMBRACE THE SCARY. USE THE FOLLOWING PAGES
TO DESCRIBE THE SADDEST, SCARIEST, AND MOST
UNCOMFORTABLE MOMENTS YOU'VE HAD ON YOUR JOURNEY.
WHAT MADE THEM SO AND HOW DID YOU CONQUER THEM?

LET'S GET PERSONAL. I THINK IN ORDER TO BREAK DOWN
BARRIERS, WE NEED TO BE COMFORTABLE DISCUSSING WHAT
THE WORLD CONSIDERED "TABOO." BUT I WANT YOU TO USE
THESE PAGES TO FILL OUT YOUR TRANSITION GOALS. GOALS
THAT CELEBRATE YOUR TRUEST SELF. AND USE THIS SPACE
TO REFLECT ON WHY YOU WANT TO ACHIEVE THESE GOALS.

LET'S TALK ABOUT YOUR FIRST KISS. HAS IT HAPPENED?
HOW WAS IT? IF IT HASN'T, HOW ARE YOU PICTURING IT?
DO YOU EVEN WANT TO HAVE A FIRST KISS? OR DID YOU
HATE IT (MINE COULD NOT HAVE BEEN MORE AWKWARD)?

COMMUNITY IS HUGELY IMPORTANT, ESPECIALLY FOR TRANS FOLKS. TAKE SOME TIME TO REFLECT ON YOUR COMMUNITY. WHO ARE THEY? HOW CAN YOU BETTER SUPPORT EACH OTHER? DO YOU WANT TO GROW YOUR COMMUNITY? IF SO, JOT DOWN A FEW IDEAS ON REACHING OUT.

FOR THE FINAL PROMPT, WE'RE GOING TO ENVISION THE FUTURE OF THE TRANS COMMUNITY. HOW DO YOU SEE THE NEXT FIVE, TEN, TWENTY, FIFTY, AND HUNDRED YEARS FOR OUR COMMUNITY SHAPING UP? PLUG INTO YOUR FAVORITE SCI FI MOVIE AND STORYBOARD YOUR LIFE AND THE WORLDS AS WE WRAP OUR FLAG AROUND THE ENTIRE PLANET. WHAT OBSTACLES ARE LEFT TO OVERCOME, WHAT NEW CHALLENGES WILL ARISE, AND WHAT VICTORIES WILL WE BE CELEBRATING?

THIS ISN'T A PROMPT SO MUCH AS SPACE FOR YOU TO
WRITE ABOUT ANYTHING YOU WANT. THOUGHTS, QUESTIONS,
FEELINGS: WHATEVER YOU NEED TO GET ON PAPER.

THIRTY-ONE DAY DOODLE CHALLENGE

I hope you found those writing exercises helpful. The idea was to get you hooked on the self-reflective therapy that writing can be. Another fantastic form of self-reflection is to doodle. We're going to use it to help you get creative and familiarize yourself with terminology you may not be familiar with. On the following pages are thirty-one topics to help inspire a doodle a day for the next month. Doodling is a wonderful way to express yourself when words just won't do. By doodling daily for a month, you'll not only learn a few new terms, but you'll discover that your art will begin to tell a story, even when you didn't think it would. For each of the words below, research them, write down the definition you have for them (or the one you found when researching it) and then doodle what comes to mind. If more than one image comes up, even better!

Acceptance

DAY 2

Ally

DAY 3

Asexual

DAY 4

Assigned at Birth

Bullying

DAY 6

Bisexual

cisgender

DAY 8

Coming Out

DAY 9

Dysphoria

Fear

Future

DAY 12

DAY 13

Gender Binary

Gender Expansive

Gender Expression

Genderfluid

Genderqueer

Homophobia

DAY 19

DAY 20

Intersex

Lesbian

DAY 22

LGBTQ+

Nonbinary

DAY 24
Outing

DAY 25

Pansexual

Queer

DAY 27

Questioning

DAY 28

Same-Gender Loving

Sexual orientation

Transgender

Transitioning

ABOUT THE AUTHOR

Milo Stewart gained a following on their YouTube channel around age seventeen because they told stories about living as a nonbinary person and that gained the attention of conservative media. Taking this reaction as a sign that their story was having an impact by challenging cisnormativity, Milo happily reclaimed the label "Social Justice Warrior" (SJW) and pursued an interest in social justice in their career.

They received a degree in Peace, Justice, and Conflict Studies from DePaul University and are working toward a master's degree in Refugee and Forced Migration Studies. They are pursuing a career helping LGBTQ+ displaced people, and Milo has funneled their academic interests into their YouTube channel, where they reflect on their experiences with gender and sexuality.

They believe in increasing access to trans and queer theory outside of academia, sharing stories of queer experiences that LGBTQ+ viewers don't get to see elsewhere in media, and building community for LGBTQ+ people of all backgrounds. Milo has had academic writings published in DePaul's undergraduate journal *Creating Knowledge* and presented a paper at the Neuchâtel Graduate Conference 2021 on Migration and Mobility Studies.

Mango Publishing, established in 2014, publishes an eclectic list of books by diverse authors—both new and established voices—on topics ranging from business, personal growth, women's empowerment, LGBTQ studies, health, and spirituality to history, popular culture, time management, decluttering, lifestyle, mental wellness, aging, and sustainable living. We were recently named 2019 *and* 2020's #1 fastest growing independent publisher by *Publishers Weekly*. Our success is driven by our main goal, which is to publish high quality books that will entertain readers as well as make a positive difference in their lives.

Our readers are our most important resource; we value your input, suggestions, and ideas. We'd love to hear from you—after all, we are publishing books for you!

Please stay in touch with us and follow us at:

Facebook: Mango Publishing
Twitter: @MangoPublishing
Instagram: @MangoPublishing
LinkedIn: Mango Publishing
Pinterest: Mango Publishing
Newsletter: mangopublishinggroup.com/newsletter

Join us on Mango's journey to reinvent publishing, one book at a time.